World Changers

2015-16 NMI
MISSION EDUCATION RESOURCES

* * *

BOOKS

WORLD CHANGERS
MKs and Where They Are Now
By Ellen Decker

EXTREME NAZARENE
Cross-Cultural Partners in Peru
By Pat Stockett Johnston

12:7 SERVE
Global Youth Serving in Mission
By David Gonzalez and Joel Tooley, Compilers

ONCE UPON AN ISLAND
From Farming to Fiji and Papua New Guinea
By Bessie Black

REVIVAL FIRES
The Horn of Africa Story
By Howie Shute

KINGDOM ADVANCE
in South Asia and India
By Dorli Gschwandtner and Sarah Dandge

* * *

NEW ADULT MISSION EDUCATION CURRICULUM
Living Mission
Where the Church Is Not Yet

World Changers

MKs and Where They are Now

Ellen Decker

Nazarene Publishing House
Kansas City, Missouri

Copyright © 2015 by Nazarene Publishing House
Nazarene Publishing House
PO Box 419527
Kansas City, MO 64141
www.BeaconHillBooks.com

ISBN 978-0-8341-3474-4

Printed in the
United States of America

Cover design: Jeff Gifford
Interior design: Sharon Page

All Scripture quotations not otherwise designated are from *The Holy
Bible, New International Version*® (NIV®). Copyright © 1973, 1978,
1984, 2011 by Biblica, Inc.™ Used by permission. All rights reserved
worldwide.

The Internet addresses, email addresses, and phone numbers
in this book are accurate at the time of publication. They are
provided as a resource. Nazarene Publishing House does not en-
dorse them or vouch for their content or permanence.

10 9 8 7 6 5 4 3 2 1

Dedication

*In loving remembrance
of grandson
Hezekiah Thason Decker*

"The LORD is my strength"

About the Author

Rev. Ellen Gailey Decker is an MK (missionary kid) from Swaziland, Africa. Ellen has lived on three continents and traveled to almost thirty countries; more than half of those have been in Africa. She is an ordained elder in the Church of the Nazarene and has served in a variety of pastoral, missions, and writing roles at the local, district, and general church levels.

Ellen is the author of three previous books—*The Power of One, Africa's Soul Hope,* and *From the Ends of the Earth*—and is the founding editor of *NCM Magazine.*

Her life verse is Acts 20:24, "I consider my life worth nothing to me; my only aim is to finish the race and complete the task the Lord Jesus has given me—the task of testifying to the good news of God's grace."

Contents

Acknowledgments

Deep appreciation goes to the fantastic missionary kids in this book who shared their hearts and lives with me. May having your past validated and recognized in this context of shared heritage give you a sense of safe homecoming.

To every MK whom I am privileged to call friend, thank you for enriching my life and the world in immeasurable ways.

Many thanks to Chuck and Doris Gailey, Sharon Lee, and Carol Holt for insights and collaboration, and to Rob, Wanda, Joshua, and Teresa Gailey for sharing a house in Swaziland with me.

With appreciation to Jeannette Brubaker, Lynn Shaw, and Wes Eby, for encouragement on the journey; and to Jeanette Littleton for excellent editing.

Thank you to Deron Matson for photographing the Southern Africa MK Reunion in San Diego in 2010, and to the Quilting Club at Mission Valley Nazarene for kindly changing their meeting date. Thank you to Dr. Daniel Ketchum for impeccable courtesy.

"Ngi swela umlomo kubonga!" [I don't have a mouth large enough to thank] my brilliant and continually amazing family: Hank; Ryan, Kendra, Alivia, Ella, Hanna; Jay, Theresa, Elias, Callum; Kevin and Lauren. Your love fuels my passion for living!

To my Friend, Jesus Christ, a TCK who forever changed my world.

Author's Notes

A third-culture kid (TCK) is a child who grows up in "neither fully the world of their parents' culture, nor fully the world of the other culture in which they were raised. In the process of living first in one dominant culture and then moving to another one, TCKs develop their own life patterns different from those who are basically born and raised in one place or culture," according to *Third Culture Kids: The Experience of Growing Up Among Worlds* by David C. Pollack and Ruth E. Van Reken.

Missionary kids (MKs) are third-culture kids, formed by the blending of two different cultures into a third culture that is uniquely theirs.

***

After an MK leaves for college, it has been the tradition of the Church of the Nazarene to pay for one trip back "home" to visit their family, if their parents are still serving on the mission field. Without exception, this trip home has been viewed as a time of healing, closure, and joy. All MKs wish to express great gladness to our denomination for its care in this regard.

Prologue
The Best Place in the World to Be

A different world cannot be built by indifferent people.
—Horace Mann

He grew up in agricultural upstate New York, never traveling far from the family farm. She grew up in Boston, daughter of a meat factory owner. He was language arts, a lover of tradition, sentimental, expressive, and philosophical. She was mathematically precise, efficient, analytical, stoic, and athletic. Collective wisdom tells us that opposites attract, and that must be true because this man and woman were different in almost every way but one: they were both wholly committed to God.

They did the right things to prepare for their call to the mission field. They graduated from Eastern Nazarene College, got married, and received their graduate degrees from Boston University and Northeastern. He pastored a church to gain ministerial experience and took additional classes at Harvard. She taught high school math followed by giving birth to two daughters.

They studied the Zulu language, updated their prayer partners, and researched African cultures.

Tragedy struck when their second daughter was just five months old. She became so ill that doctors ran out of unhindered veins and had to inject medicine into her head. Her lung collapsed and she was on oxygen to breathe. Their baby girl's leg was sliced open to insert a feeding tube. The father cried out to God in anguish, "Please, hasn't she suffered enough?" She was transferred to the best children's hospital in Boston, one of the best in the world.

All to no avail.

The doctors called the parents in to see their child one last time to say good-bye. The parents called the church to ask for prayer, and then they knelt to pray. The young mother did not ask why. Softly, she thanked God for giving them a beautiful little girl for five wonderful months.

The world-renowned medical staff could not understand it. The child they had given up for dead was slowly, unbelievably showing signs of life.

A year later the family was packed and ready for Africa. Though alive, their little girl often had serious bouts of illness. A concerned friend took the young parents aside and admonished them, "Why are you still determined to go to Africa? Don't you think

God wants you to take care of your family? Why would He give you a sickly child if He really wanted you to go? You are giving up the best medical care in the world to take her to rural Africa. Mark my words, you will go with two daughters and return with one!"

They went to Africa anyway.

The couple in this true story is my mom and dad, Doris and Chuck Gailey. I was that deathly ill child—whom God miraculously healed during their first year as missionaries in Swaziland, Africa, in 1964.

Like Shadrach, Meshach, and Abednego in Daniel 3, my parents begged for a miracle. "Please heal our child before we leave for Africa," they prayed—but if not, they were going to serve God anyway. They knew, sickly child or not, that the best place in the world to be is the center of God's will.

I have often wondered, *What if?* What if my parents heeded the advice of their friend and stayed in Boston for my medical care? Would God still have miraculously healed me? Or was that perhaps an honor and blessing for these obedient followers of Christ? We may never know. The lasting legacy of my missionary parents is simply this: God first.

Yet as I have traveled the world and spoken to countless Nazarenes and preached at Faith Promise conventions, one of the saddest refrains I have heard repeatedly is this: "I am called to missions, and I want to serve God, *but what about my children?* I just don't think I can raise them on the mission field." There is a myth out there that being raised on the mission field is a subpar experience for children.

Quite the contrary.

Being raised as a third-culture kid actually has proven benefits, as you will quickly see from the stories in this book. Many missionary kids not only survive their childhood mission experiences but thrive—so much so that many are now involved in life-changing ministries as adults. Our endeavors in Nazarene missions don't just end when a missionary retires. It is an ongoing investment in the lives of the next generation—and the next and the next.

Join me on a journey exploring a transformational Christian worldview that comes from growing up in multiple cultures. Discover what missionary kids learned while growing up on the mission field—and how those experiences metamorphosed them into devoted servants of Christ. Rejoice as you taste the fruit of Nazarene missions. Be renewed as you encounter these world changers who have taken up the mantle and motto of their radically obedient missionary parents: God first.

1
Mission to the World

The whole course of human history may depend on a change of heart in one solitary and even humble individual—for it is in the solitary mind and soul of the individual that the battle between good and evil is waged and ultimately won or lost.
—M. Scott Peck

I once visited a refugee camp in Africa. People were so surprised to see a white woman, modestly dressed, who would come to visit them. All of the children crowded around and begged to have their pictures taken with me. But my memories of that place don't require a photograph; they are imprinted forever on my mind.

* * *

As a fourteen-year-old MK in Africa, Helen Noble* told her mom, "God is preparing me to do something other people would consider difficult, but He reassured me that He will be with me."

At eighteen, as Helen prepared to leave Africa for college, she heard the song, "Keep Your Candle Burning," which talks about continuing to serve the Lord when we're discouraged and one person making a difference. God spoke to Helen again, this time asking her to keep her candle burning in Africa.

Thinking God was calling her to medical missions, Helen decided to pursue a biochemistry major. Although she was president of MuKappa (a society for MKs), Helen struggled with her new culture.

"Two things helped me through those tough college years. First, my mom set up a daily time—12 noon for me and 7 p.m. for them—when we prayed for each other. She reassured me that the Spirit of God could join us together and somehow, over ten thousand miles, He did.

"Second, my job gave me one free fax a week. Being able to update my parents on my life on a weekly basis brought comfort."

When Helen couldn't get into medical school, her "missionary uncle," Dr. Charles (Chuck) Gailey, encouraged her to attend Nazarene Theological Seminary (NTS) to study missiology. Helen took several missions classes but earned a master's degree in divinity after discovering how much she loved learning and teaching theology. While at NTS Helen met her husband, a follower of Christ from a country in Africa that was resistant to the gospel.

"Emmanuel's father was a leader in a non-Christian religion who expected his son to follow in his footsteps," she explains. "But at age fifteen Emmanuel heard the gospel on the radio. For the next three years he read the Bible through each year and then decided to follow Christ."

Seven years passed before Emmanuel found a like-minded believer in his country to help him begin a house church. They were up to fourteen members in the church—a megachurch in a country that persecutes Christians!—when they were betrayed.

Emmanuel fled to a neighboring country. There a follower of Christ invited him to church, and Emmanuel fell in love with the Nazarenes.

"While I was dating Emmanuel I was blessed to have the godly counsel of 'Uncle' Chuck and 'Aunt' Doris. I had not grown up around people of other major world religions, so I knew there would be cultural differences. Then I had to deal with those who were worried about my living and serving in a country where Christians are persecuted, saying it is not safe.

"Really? If God is calling you, even to a place others think is dangerous, that's the safest place for you to be. As long as we are going by the will and the grace and in the presence of the Overcomer, we know we are in the right place."

Everyday life in the country where Emmanuel and Helen currently serve is challenging. She makes bread daily. Canned products are expensive, so everything has to be peeled, seeded, minced, pounded, and chopped. Thankfully, they do have electricity, at least from 6 a.m. until midnight, and every other day from March to September. Emmanuel and Helen's typical monthly "date" is to travel two hours to the major city for a grocery shopping excursion without the kids. They have a daily helper to clean and do their shopping at the local marketplace. That way Helen doesn't have to go with the four youngest children or pay double because she is American.

"I would probably not be doing what I am doing if I hadn't been an MK," she reflects. "I am amazed at how God prepared me for this lifestyle. For instance, I had to wear dresses while growing up, so I can easily accept the modest clothing I must wear now. As a child I shared mealie pap, a cornmeal porridge, out of a communal bowl with friends. Today I dip bread or rice into sauces or meats as we eat with neighbors. I often wear my hair covered, just as married ladies did where I grew up.

"In this culture, if Emmanuel did the dishes, people would mutter what a bad wife he has. People would not respect him enough to listen to the gospel. But when we travel in the US, he helps a lot with household and parenting chores. Being an MK has also helped me tremendously since I learned to quickly let people into my life but I also learned to be willing to quickly let them go, and that is useful as a missionary."

From a conduct standpoint, Emmanuel and Helen enjoy raising their six children—Hillela, Faustina, Oliver, Akyra, Camilia, and Caden—in a more conservative culture. They don't have to worry about underwear or belly buttons showing because people are modest. People in this religion generally don't drink alcohol and they highly discourage premarital sex. Their TV stations edit out the swearing and rarely even show a kiss.

But raising the children as Christians is more challenging.

"We have to be careful when they play with other children in the neighborhood because of what they may say about our Christian practices and beliefs. That tends to be pretty isolating. Fortunately we have some Christian friends we can welcome into the sanctuary of our home. One of these is an or-

Helen Noble with refugee children

dained elder, a district superintendent who was shot in the stomach and almost died. When he comes in the door my kids shriek with joy because Adeer (Uncle) Mohammed has come to visit."

The primary responsibility Emmanuel and Helen have is to disciple and train the new believers from a different religious background who are learning to become leaders and evangelists. Helen wrote a basic curriculum called "The Emmaus Road Course" that is being used throughout Africa. Through five units, of five hours each, it trains leaders in Bible, theology, history of the church, administration and finance, and how to become a Nazarene.

"Fellowship with the new believers from different religious backgrounds is the highlight of our ministry. For security reasons, we don't usually have more than ten people gather at a time. Our biggest stress comes from concern for our leaders. One pastor was poisoned because of his faith and his skin began to peel off. Yet when he left the hospital, he went back to pastor his church.

"Another pastor was shot six times with an AK-47 and left for dead. Within a month he was miraculously walking again. The prayers of Nazarenes around the world help us see healing that defies the medical community. And when Nazarenes have been martyred, prayer has helped the people come to Christ, so that we now have more than sixty house churches in this country."

Helen is convinced that if God calls you to do something, He will equip you to do it. And that's the way she lives. She has three major goals in life: to raise her children to say yes to whatever the Lord wants them to do, to live in various Muslim countries and share Christ, and to get a PhD in Islamic studies.

"Sadly, sometimes we forget that God loves the world and He wants *all* to be saved. If we ignore more than a billion people in another major world religion, we are neglecting our mission to the world. I once met a lady in her sixties who told me that God called her to be a missionary when she was twelve. But then she got married, had kids, and never went. And I thought, *What a wasted life. What did she do that was so important that she couldn't give God her all?* None of her kids was following the Lord. If parents disobey, chances are that at a critical moment in their life, their kids will disobey too. "I am thankful for my wonderful parents and our church leaders that encourage our obedience to do what God called us to do. The Church of the Nazarene is by far one of the best mission organizations in existence. We balance each other, keep each other accountable, and help each other grow to our fullest potential. Emmanuel and I deeply appreciate how churches support our ministry through the World Evangelism Fund and through prayers."

Helen Noble has lived in South, East, and West Africa and has visited Central Africa. She is more convinced than ever that we as a church need to focus more on reaching people from other religious traditions.

"We need to encourage people to hear God's call to them, to train them for effective ministry in these challenging areas and to send them, trusting the Lord to keep them safe."

Helen and her family are leading by example, courageously involved in God's mission to the world.

Most names in this chapter have been changed for security purposes.

2

World Cure

Success means that I am able to carry my values into the world, that I am able to change it in positive ways.
—Maxine Hong Kingston

In a famous poem by Robert Frost, "Birches," Frost talks about a young boy riding his father's trees by swinging them down over and over again.

We didn't have birch trees in Swaziland, but there was nothing better than parachuting down the wattle trees on the Endzingeni mission station. I'd scramble quickly up the smooth gray trunk, climbing higher and higher toward heaven, and then launch myself out on the perfect limb.

The arching branch would propel me down faster and faster. At just the right moment, I'd let go and return triumphantly to earth. I still bear the chipped tooth from my early tries. Still, a person could do worse than be a parachuter of wattles.

Dr. Douglas (Doug) Evans, a graduate of Oklahoma State University College of Osteopathic Medicine and a pediatrician in St. Joseph, Missouri, vividly remembers the day he decided to become a medical doctor.

"Once a month a doctor from the Nazarene hospital in Manzini, Swaziland, would split his day serving patients in Endzingeni and the nearby town of Pigg's Peak. One day Dr. Paul Sutherland chugged up the mountain in his old Peugeot and offered to let me watch him work. Ever since that day all I wanted to be was a physician, and I thought I would be a surgeon."

Doug was just six years old.

With no TV and poor radio reception, Doug found other ways to entertain himself. He learned to play guitar and did a lot of hiking, climbing, and bike riding. At age fifteen he rode his bike alone from Pietermaritzburg, South Africa, to Siteki, Swaziland, a total of four hundred miles over five days. Doug traveled with just a spare inner tube, spanner, change of underwear, and about $10USD in his pocket. He stayed one night in a small hotel, one night with friends, one night in a police barracks, and one night with a local chief of police.

Dr. Doug Evans after bike ride from PMB

Around these adventurous activities Doug felt drawn to helping others. At seventeen, he spent his school vacation observing and assisting the missionary doctors in surgery, in the emergency room, and by delivering babies at Raleigh Fitkin Memorial Hospital. His early years were also influenced by missionaries Larry Edgerton and Dr. Samuel Hynd.

Doug was also impacted by some tough times and heartache. At a government boarding school the head boy lied to the matron about Doug, and Doug was beaten with a leather strap. Tragically, systematic abuse occurred in the institution. Years later, those memories still affected Doug's life.

"About halfway through a two-month medical internship at a hospital in Oklahoma, my wife, Dawn, and our two small boys came for a visit. As they were leaving around the corner of the hospital, I had a sudden flashback to my parents driving away after leaving me at boarding school. I was instantly overwhelmed with a deep sense of being left 'again,' and I went to my room where I cried for more than an hour. I began to realize what a significant role MKs have in missionary work, and how important healthy and well-functioning children are to a family's overall well-being."

Doug decided to enter pediatrics. Today he runs a successful professional practice with a nurse practitioner and support staff. But Doug sees a direct correlation between his values today and the challenges he faced as a child.

When the head boy who caused his beatings showed up at the airport to say good-bye in 1977, Doug held no malice. He chose to extend the hand of forgiveness to his enemy.

As an employer, he shuns the negative and reinforces people positively by complimenting good efforts. In 2010 when Doug experienced a heart attack and needed five coronary bypasses, his staff gladly went the extra mile for their kind and thoughtful boss. Though half his patients are on Medicaid, Doug can treat each one with dignity and respect because he lived among poverty.

"I was only home in short bursts on school holidays, but my parents taught me wonderful values. Tolerance, patience, obedience, to never tell a lie; all lessons that helped me raise my three sons, Michael, Kyle, and Daniel. When I went to Bethany College, which is now Southern Nazarene University, no one told me to turn off the TV or to study. Yet the discipline instilled in childhood sustained me through twelve years of school and training to become a doctor."

Fellow MKs also contributed to Doug's life. Pearl Hetrick Campbell taught him his first song on the guitar, and brother Dan honed Doug's guitar skills. Today Doug uses that skill in worship at his church. Another MK, Cindy Human Bryant, introduced Doug to her friend Dawn. Doug and Dawn were married in 1980. Doug still keeps in touch with childhood MK friends, hosting MK reunions in his home.

"Unlike many MKs, I have been able to return to Africa only once, on a Work and Witness trip in 2005. I reconnected with old friends and spent an evening reminiscing with Dr. Hynd. We discussed HIV/AIDS and the current status of treatment available for the people of Swaziland; as physicians we all hope for a world cure.

"Across from me on Dr. Hynd's office wall was a piece of string art I had made for him twenty-eight years before. I realized then why every time I walk into a Nazarene church I feel like I am with family. We *are* family! That is the greatness of an MK heritage."

Doug's sister, MK Shelley Evans Coil, agrees.

"No matter where I go in the world, I see someone who knows my family or we discover a mutual acquaintance. Being an MK gives a person an ability to see the big picture, how God weaves details and experiences together and connects all the threads. In fact, my life is a direct result of my parents' obedience to God, since observing a family on the mission field led to my parents' decision to have their fifth child, me."

Besides homeschooling her children, Madison, Regan, and Sawyer (Sara is in college on a soccer scholarship), and attending their national horse competitions, Shelley is involved in inner-city ministry in Oklahoma City through her church, Bethany First Church of the Nazarene (BFCN). At women's retreats, Shelley testifies of God's peace during her 2009 bout with breast cancer. She is a gifted soloist, sometimes singing in Siswati, the local language of Swaziland.

"Swaziland was my people, my language, my experience. I was born there, and it was really hard to go to the Philippines when my parents were reassigned when I was ten. I soon learned that all people have the same needs, no matter what the color of skin or where the location in the world.

"Unfortunately, the climate there disagreed with my mom, and she was sick a lot. So when I was thirteen I faced the challenge of adapting to US culture. I lived here for thirty-one years before I had opportunity to go home again."

That opportunity came through BFCN and their ten-year missional partnership with Swaziland. The BFCN is working alongside the Swazi Nazarenes in their clinics, churches, and schools—particularly with at-risk children and the AIDS crisis. Shelley joined their first GO (Global Outreach) Team in 2008.

"Our compassionate ministry team worked with coordinators Mary Magagula and Evelyn Shongwe. We delivered food, supplies, and prayer to people living

Shelley with a Swazi child 2013

with AIDS. I was saddened by the number of people dying. A bright spot was visiting New Hope Center, an orphanage managed by a fellow MK, Dr. Elizabeth Hynd. Though they can only serve about fifty children out of one hundred thousand orphans in the country, there is an atmosphere of hope as they work toward raising Christian leaders for Swaziland's future.

"Another highlight was seeing Mfundisi (Rev.) Pato. As he began to speak in Siswati, I was unexpectedly swept back to hearing him many times in tent revivals when I was a little girl. Though old and frail, he was still preaching and serving the Lord. Tears rolled down my dusty cheeks as I realized God is still very much at work in Swaziland."

Shelley's first trip cemented in her a desire to return as frequently as possible to minister there. She went on another GO Team in 2010, this time with her daughter Regan. In 2013 she traveled with twenty US musicians and Swazi Nazarenes, performing in a series of AIDS Awareness Music Festivals across Swaziland. She hopes that someday her entire family can go to Swaziland together.

"I want my legacy to be a clear reliance on God's sovereignty," Shelley explains. "The biggest gift we can ever give our children is allowing them to see their parents act in obedience to Jesus Christ. I am so grateful my parents lived what they preached. They loved people. At home they were kind to their children. Nothing was inconsistent between what they said and what they did.

"All of those things instill confidence, stability, and a sense of worth in a child, no matter where you live. Even though my parents had hard times, and my mom struggled with illness, throughout sixty years of marriage they have lived the holiness lifestyle of sacrificial love. That is what the gospel is all about."

From the US to Swaziland, Dr. Doug Evans and Shelley Evans Coil are bringing physical and spiritual healing to hundreds of children.

3

The Edge of the World

Life is either a daring adventure or nothing. To keep our faces toward change and behave like free spirits is strength undefeatable.
—Helen Keller

One day our truck got stuck in heavy wet sand up to the bottom of the chassis. We were on a little bush road, stranded at the edge of the world. No amount of digging could rescue us. A Swazi boy with four scrawny oxen said he could pull us out. I was skeptical.

After hooking the oxen up to the truck, the boy whistled and cracked his whip over their heads. The cattle lunged forward and the truck sucked right up out of the sand. Seconds later the oxen leaped up the steep three-foot-high edge of the wadi, dragging the bouncing truck right up after them. Dad was so impressed and grateful that he gave the boy his favorite pocketknife.

❊ ❊ ❊

Identical twins Todd and Tom Nothstine arrived in Africa at the age of five. Climbing into the car at the airport, one of them exclaimed, "Look, the steering wheel is on the wrong side!" to which the other replied, "Oh, it'll be OK once we get turned around!"

The ride of their lives had just begun.

Todd and Tom were adventurous kids, and Africa was filled with endless possibilities. They spent hours playing in their tree house, riding bikes, and hiking through the Lebombo Mountains.

Inspired by the Silver Creek Gang books, they went fishing with their freshly cut cane poles, string, and paper clip hooks. They raised two wild owls, Screechy I and II, from ugly downy ball chicks to mature birds. The boys raided honeycombs until the dreadful sound of deep humming from thousands of bees moving in a shadowy mass made them run for their lives.

"One day we were hiking in a dense, lonely ravine, past a series of picturesque little pools, still and ink-black in the shadows. At the bottom of the granite slope lay a scattering of fresh peelings from wild fruit.

"Suddenly a mighty *RAW!* shattered the cool silence of the ravine. Heard from a distance, the ferocious bark of a baboon is a thrillingly wild sound of

37

the African bush. Heard at close range, it is terrifying. My brother and I ran faster than we ever had. When we reached the top of the ravine, breathless and panting, we could see the troop of baboons. Thankfully, they weren't chasing us!

"A close second to this experience was the time we each had big sticks and were trying to rout a cobra out of a pile of cinder blocks near our trash pit. In the frenzy of flailing sticks, Tom clobbered me over the head. That took me out of the action for a moment. As my head cleared I felt a spray hit my right arm. The cobra was defending itself, but fortunately its venom missed my eyes."

Both Tom and Todd have degrees in biology from Olivet Nazarene University and play musical instruments, but their MK experiences hardwired adventure and a love of the outdoors into them. They went to the edge of Alaska where they have worked in a cannery, a construction firm, and commercial fishing. Their jobs have ranged from one-hundred-hour workweeks on the cannery "slime line" cleaning pink salmon, to working as deckhands on fishing boats. During his turn at wheel watch one dark night, Tom just barely saved their boat from ramming an iceberg. Orcas have swum so close to their boat that they could have stepped off the deck onto the killer whales' backs.

In construction, Tom escaped certain death when a trench collapsed where he had been lying, eyeballing the grade, just seconds before; another time he barely avoided having twelve thousand pounds of rocks dumped on him. When a black bear wandered onto their worksite, the twins simply "shooed him off."

Both prefer adventure, and shudder at the thought of a desk job. Todd, an outstanding photographer, loves to post pictures of glaciers, mountains, and other scenic vistas as his description of his work on his Facebook page.

Tom working on a rig in Alaska

"Dad taught us that part of being a Christian and holding a biblical worldview means being an employee of integrity and hard work. I know I am fortunate to be employed and to have the opportunity to move between jobs at will. Having seen economies in less developed countries firsthand, it is impossible for me to take my economically privileged existence for granted."

Tom agrees.

"From the shoes on my feet to a cold, clean glass of water from the faucet, I think of my Swazi friends—many of them carrying water from a pond or coming to church barefoot—and I know I'm rich. I also know that more things, more stuff, nicer stuff, newer stuff, will not and cannot bring true happiness or contentment. That's the perspective on life that being an MK gave me."

Tom and Todd love the benefits of being MKs: cross-cultural experience, travel, exposure to other languages, the special missionary "family," a greater appreciation of friends (because you know the reality of having to say good-bye), a childhood largely shielded from moral garbage, a Christian worldview that is not ethnocentric, a real gratefulness for the abundance and opportunity that exists in the US, an appreciation for fellow believers around the world, and rich and interesting life experiences because Africa was their home.

Today Todd and Tom still look alike, have an insatiable thirst for adventure, and work for the same construction company in Alaska. Both say their parents have been an inspiration with their commitment to the Lord, to each other, and as missionaries. Yet their lives are very different.

Tom married Nicole in August 2002.

"We were thrilled when Nicole became pregnant. When a routine ultrasound revealed the baby's brain had failed to develop, we were devastated. Over the months we were deeply touched by the prayers of people around the world. By the time our precious Natalia was born, we had peace in our hearts and a deep love for her. Natalia was blind and required a feeding tube. She was beautiful! Sadly, she lived only a few weeks.

"During this time the significance of the song 'Because He Lives' became fiercely real to us. The song talks about how we can endure all things because Christ lives and mentions that we feel joy in holding a newborn knowing the calm assurance that the child can face uncertainty because Jesus lives. This song is no less real as we raise our five healthy, wonderful children: Vincent, Thomas, twins Isabelle and Victoria, and Genevieve."

One of Tom's goals is to take his family to see where he grew up in Africa, to experience that special place that still runs deep in his veins. In the meantime, Tom serves on the church board at Cordova Church of the Nazarene and leads the teen Sunday school class. During their pastoral search Tom filled in on the preaching rotation.

"The first time I preached I spoke on a Christian worldview; that English is not God's first language and God isn't Caucasian. Christianity isn't about having a divine right to health and wealth. Think of it this way: if a gospel preached to a wealthy megachurch congregation would be absurd to a poor third-world congregation, then it's a false gospel."

Todd, on the other hand, works construction and commercial fishing in Alaska for only five months of the year. Four months of the year he basically lives on a boat on the Great Salt Lake in Utah, harvesting Brine Shrimp roe, which most people recognize as the Sea Monkeys advertised on the back of comic books. The other three months of the year he visits his sister Tricia in Washington, their parents in Illinois, and travels the world. He has gone canyoning (rappelling down a river gorge and jumping into pools) in Reunion, ridden horseback in Swaziland, explored caves in Madagascar, bungee-jumped near Hobbiton in New Zealand, photographed the jeweled cityscape of Tel Aviv at night, joined a Work and Witness team in Costa Rica, and jumped out of a plane over Hawaii.

"My most memorable worship experiences were in Israel. I stayed in a hostel on the Red Sea that had a Christian service on Friday night in the courtyard. About one hundred of us sang and worshipped in five or six languages—it was amazing. Another day I attended a service where we sang in Hebrew and a Messianic Jew preached on why Christ is the Messiah. Heaven is going to be awesome!"

When traveling, Todd meticulously researches the best airfare, stays in hostels, eats mostly roadside food, and uses public transport. Even at home in Alaska, all his belongings could fit in the back of a pickup truck.

"I don't own much. My treasures are seeing God's creation and meeting new people—experiences more valuable than mere things. Of course, some experiences you don't want to have, like the time I accidentally locked myself out of my room in Paris. I had been using the bathroom down the hall and had nothing but a towel . . ."

Todd Nothstine and the plane he flew in South Africa

Todd's life goals include climbing Mount Kilimanjaro, scuba diving, memorizing large portions of Scripture, and going on more Work and Witness trips. When he is in Alaska, he serves as an adult Sunday school substitute teacher, plays the guitar, and has led the missions lessons for years.

As young adults, both Todd and Tom returned to South Africa where they attended flight school and learned how to fly small planes. Today their love of adventure and witness for Christ is still soaring high.

4
The World Is a Book

Travel is more than the seeing of sights;
it is a change that goes on, deep and permanent,
in the ideas of the living.
—Miriam Beard

My early years were spent in the garden of Eden: Arthurseat, South Africa. We kids had an important job to do: keeping the goats out of the garden. Most days we grabbed our sticks and chased those goats through the overgrown grass. We would pretend they were lions or antelopes and patrol the bush. Those unfortunate enough to fall into our hands were penned up until the owners came to sheepishly collect them. As a nurse who had treated herd boys gored by goats, Mom always gave us strict instructions to be careful. Mostly, I think she just prayed a lot.

* * *

Frances Elizabeth (Beth) Restrick was probably destined to lead a global life before she was born. Her parents met and married in Swaziland, where her British mother was a maternity nurse at Raleigh Fitkin Memorial Hospital and her American father was a Peace Corps volunteer at the Manzini Nazarene High School. By the time Beth was thirteen, she had lived eighteen months to four years in each of six countries: US, England, South Africa, Swaziland, Portugal, and Mozambique. She was just twelve when her family moved to Mozambique, where her life changed forever.

"I went from the garden of Arthurseat and the wide open spaces of Swaziland to the city of Maputo. Our neighbors stared down from their apartments into our tiny walled-in yard. A kiosk sold beer across the street. My sister, Mary, and I played our music loudly to drown out the sounds of gunshot and drunken brawls. I saw a woman being stabbed to death in the driveway next door to us. I felt bewildered and lost.

"Around this time my mom introduced me to the *Lord of the Rings* trilogy. Not only was it an escape from the events around me, but it reminded me to stand firm in the battle of good and evil. As a teen stretching toward adulthood, the 'orcs' I battled were those of not knowing Portuguese and desperately needing friends at an age when relationships are critical.

"Our pastor at Maputo Central Nazarene, Rev. Bessie Tshambe, took the time to notice a lonely MK. She asked Mrs. Gloria Macie to visit us with her two children, Joinha and Nito. Soon they came over every day after school. We played basketball and did puzzles. After a while I dreaded hearing them knocking on the gate and trying to think of something new to do that didn't require our knowing each other's language!

"Then we began to sing hymns from the Portuguese and Shangaan hymnbooks over and over. I began to pick up phrases, expressions, tone, and inflection. One day I realized I loved Mozambique.

"I joined the youth choir of eighty kids—I was the only foreigner—and we went on a retreat to rural Manjacaze. We slept on the ground in an unfinished church with no roof and a nearby pit toilet. During the times of fellowship around the fires, singing, marching (we called it the Shangaan Shuffle), and looking at the Milky Way together . . . the cultural barriers melted away.

"I will never forget the time of unity when we praised the Lord together and became one under the starry African sky. South Africa and Swaziland are special, but Mozambique fuels my passion and love for Africa as an adult. That's where I developed deep roots with the people, and Joinha is still my best friend today."

Beth's love of Africa and her childhood visits to see the wild animals in Kruger National Park in South Africa inspired her to want to be a game ranger. While attending Eastern Nazarene College, she signed up for a summer wildlife management course in Kenya. Three months before the class she realized she had money for airfare, but not tuition. She agonized in prayer, giving her future and her situation to God. The *very next* day the financial aid office called to say there had been an overpayment in her bill, enough to cover her tuition!

"I should have known with that miracle that God really wanted me there. I had longed to work with the animals, but instead got stuck interviewing local villagers about the impact of animals on their lives. Because they cannot afford fences, the men often sleep in their fields. They bang on pots to scare animals away.

"At one homestead we were sent to the field where the husband stood, distraught. A herd of elephants had devastated his crop the night before.

He was anguished over how he was going to feed his family. No crops also meant no school fees for his children. Suddenly I realized—animals are wonderful, but this was one of God's children! My priorities began to change."

Upon graduation from ENC, Beth volunteered for a year in Mozambique. The Bible college desperately needed a regular library for accreditation. They had boxes of books and Beth rose to the challenge, writing out every title, author, and book number by hand. Her dad made shelves, and later Beth computerized the inventory. When Beth left, the library had seventeen hundred volumes and was a popular place to hang out.

"That year was life-changing for me. To have students tell me they long to keep learning, and to have to say to their tears, 'I'm sorry, I cannot give you even one book; we must keep them for future students.' It is heartbreaking to deny someone a book! Many had to walk miles each week to copy verses from a neighboring pastor's Bible. I think it is hard for people to comprehend the lack of literature in so many places in Africa—and the critical importance of projects like NMI's Books for Pastors, or the wonderful Nazarene-led ministry Christian Literature for Africa (www.christianlitforafrica.org)."

Beth returned to Boston with a new passion. She enrolled at Simmons University for a master's degree in Library Science and became a library assistant at Boston University's Library of African Studies. Just four years later, despite being extremely young for the job, Beth was promoted to head librarian.

"I absolutely love my job with the beautiful view of the Charles River. I thought I knew a lot about the continent, but with access to two hundred thousand books on Africa, I realize I have so much more to learn! We are open to the public, although we primarily have students, faculty, and scholars from around the world. Our imported newspapers really draw Africans in, hungry to read news of home. Many of them are working or studying long hours and are incredibly lonely. My MK experiences help me to empathize with them. In His amazing way, God has uniquely placed me in a location for outreach to people from all over Africa."

Outside of work, Beth's love of Africa is expressed through her vivid, beautiful paintings of wild animals, people, and scenery in Africa. Her paintings are sought after, and her best are printed into note cards. She also paints African animals or scenes on necklaces and paperweight rocks.

Using her gift for ministry, Beth has designed Africa's Child Sponsorship Christmas cards, posters, centerpieces, and large displays for local and district NMI conventions. Sometimes she draws unique coloring sheets for the thirty-five kids she teaches missions to every month at Wollaston Nazarene Church.

Beth also speaks at churches for Faith Promise weekends. Another unique ministry Beth has is collecting, cleaning, and sending used "disposable" Communion cups. Today Nazarene Bible College graduates in Mozambique receive a Bible, Nazarene *Manual*, and one hundred Communion cups.

Beth has taken four levels of Zulu classes at Boston University, and in 2007 her class sang for Bishop Desmond Tutu. She has spoken about African conservation at ENC and volunteered at the local Franklin Zoo.

"Volunteering at the zoo highlights another advantage of being an MK. People see my animation about the animals. This leads to discovering I grew up in Africa, why my parents went, and my Christian faith. Having an MK childhood opens up the world."

Beth has returned to Africa five times as an adult. In 2011 she volunteered at the Southern Wildlife College in South Africa and was delighted to discover that many of the African staff were Nazarenes.

Beth Restrick with two Masaai warriors

When Beth's parents retired in 2013, she went back to Africa to say good-bye to home as she knew it. It was a poignant journey. When Beth boarded the jumbo jet to wing her way back to America, Ladysmith Black Mambazo's song "Homeless" was playing over the speakers. Beth began to cry at the heartbreak of leaving Africa behind, perhaps for good. A storm was brewing to the north and as the plane took off in that direction, Beth was able to pick out the Nazarene Seminary of Mozambique, though it was hard to see through her tears. As the plane turned and the seminary disappeared from sight, Beth lifted her face to the sky, and there before her was a brilliant rainbow—she felt that for her, it was a promise from the Lord that He is still in control.

Beth longs to return someday, and her growing dream is for community centers in Africa. These would draw together her three loves: library (Christian books for the local culture), environment (animals and trees), and art (helping local artists engage in self-sustaining projects). She is active on the Africana Librarians Council and also serves on a committee that decides which organizations should receive funds for building libraries in Africa. She recently hosted the director of the Lubuto Library Project in Zambia. The Lubuto project promotes libraries as community educational centers that provide a safe haven for youth. Beth hopes that someday she is part of taking this concept into Mozambique.

"Being an MK is the lens through which I view my world. I have been blessed with spiritually strong women who loved and mentored me. Foremost is my mom, who is the most selfless person I know. Then there is Marjorie Stockwell, a blind, retired missionary who simply loved a homesick MK. And Pastor

Tshambe—even when I couldn't understand her language, I sensed the Holy Spirit when she preached. And my grandmother was like a second mom to me.

"These four modeled for me that missions is a lifestyle. We are all called to global evangelism—whether we go and tell or stay and support. Augustine once said, 'The world is a book, and those who do not travel read only a page.' Participation in world evangelism enables us to read more of the book."

From Mozambique to Boston, Beth's witness for the Lord is giving many a new chapter on life.

5

Whirled View

Education is the most powerful weapon
which you can use to change the world.
—Nelson Mandela

Bees lived in an old, abandoned, wooden box in the
eucalyptus woods behind our home in Siteki. When you
lifted the lid, their golden treasure gleamed.

I am allergic to bees, but that didn't stop me from
going in there with a smoking wad of newspaper, grabbing
those honeycombs, and running. I would suck out the vel-
vety sweetness until I was sick as a dog. It was wonderful!

* * *

Dr. William (Bill) Hetrick is a professor and the
department chair of Psychological and Brain Sciences
at Indiana University. His credentials are impressive:
BA in psychology from Point Loma Nazarene University (PLNU); MA in experimental psychology from

California State University Fullerton; PhD in Clinical Psychology from Ohio State University; an internship in clinical psychology at Harvard's McLean Hospital in Boston; six years at the University of California Irvine Psychiatry Department researching autism and self-injurious behavior; and recipient of million-dollar federal research grants to study schizophrenia and bipolar disorder at Indiana University, Bloomington. And to think Bill's inquisitive nature began as a young child in a simple mud hut . . .

"My Swazi friends and I made our own mud bricks and built a mud hut. One day we discovered an old car battery that still had some juice in it. So we figured out how to wire it to a flashlight bulb. With just a switch, we could bring light into our mud hut. Today I am trying to figure out the electrical signals that underlie the complexities of the human mind. And for those whose electrical signals are misfiring, I'm trying to discover if there are ways to find a switch that could help them."

As a child, Bill had other important things on his mind too. Taking care of his pet baboon, Tsotsi, for example, or riding the wild donkeys that wandered onto the mission station. He made slingshots and tree houses, ate roasted grasshoppers, raised chickens and ducks, and fished in the local pond without disturbing the resident hippo. More than one time Bill reached into tall grass or a weaver bird's nest and accidentally disturbed a sleeping puff adder or green mamba.

"It's amazing I survived my childhood! Yet that was nothing compared to the 'danger' I sensed as a twelve-year-old transitioning to the US. I felt pure Swazi and was upset about leaving my home behind. One day Pastor Earl Lee invited my dad and me to a Dodger's baseball game. I thought it was a stupid thing to hit a ball and run around in circles, so I went grudgingly. As we walked in, the announcer's voice boomed through the stadium and I heard a huge roar from the crowd. Instantly I was transported to my backyard in Swaziland, listening to the South African Kaizer Chiefs soccer games on a tiny AM radio under a tree. Different sport, different clothes, different people, but that same roar of the crowd carried me into this culture. To this day, I love baseball!"

As a teen in Pasadena, California, Bill's job was to drive around greater L.A., delivering psychological reports for a clinic. While collating the reports, he became curious about psychological assessment and the workings of the mind. His fascination with people's personalities and patterns of behavior grew, and he chose to major in psychology at PLNU. Professors there had a profound impact on Bill.

"In all the years I heard my father preach, he always said there was nothing insurmountable that could not be matched by the greater grace of Jesus. Professor Keith Holly allowed me to integrate my childhood upbringing about grace with psychologist Carl Rogers' view of unconditional positive regard. Professor Gene Mallory challenged us to consider God as a creative God, instrumental in the creative process around us."

As part of that creative process, Bill and his research team directly study people suffering from schizophrenia and bipolar disorder, as well as healthy, unaffected individuals. They study what causes hallucinations or delusions, those whirled mix-ups in the mental process.

Bill uses a variety of behavioral, cognitive, and neural methods to test the theory that schizophrenia may be caused by a lack of fluid coordination in the brain. Essentially, he and his colleagues try to figure out brain mechanisms that are associated with the development, progression, and maintenance of functional and dysfunctional brain processes. Besides research, Bill teaches and mentors students working toward their doctorates in psychological and brain sciences. Bill has a unique and—judging by the number of his students who have won national awards—successful approach to research.

"There is a tendency in academia to work alone. Because I grew up in the Swazi culture, which is more community-oriented than individualistic, I emphasized collaborative research.

"The Swazi culture also shows great respect for elders and family lineage. Accordingly, I have great interest in academic lineage, for the scientists who paved the way for the present generation of investigators and for training the next generation of explorers.

"I find a lot of ideas like this are a tremendous benefit of intertwining two cultures, a distinct advantage for any MK. A future dream of mine is to be involved in global mental health issues, to strengthen the application of behavioral and social sciences in less privileged countries. My desire to serve was deeply instilled during my MK years."

Bill and his high school sweetheart, Carol, are parents of daughters Alexandra and Gabrielle. Along with Bill's sister Lynda and her family, they all traveled to Swaziland in 2006. They came away with a renewed passion for Swaziland and its amazing, resilient people.

Lynda, a whirling dynamo of energy and enthusiasm, loves people and has the gift of inspiring

**Paul Hetrick, Gabbie Hetrick, Bill Hetrick
in Swaziland 2013**

them to service. She began to ask the Lord what she could do for Him in Swaziland. With grandparents, parents, and two aunts who served as missionaries in Africa, Lynda already understood the Swazi culture and how things functioned. Her missionary grandfather used to say, "I didn't come to teach the Swazis but to walk alongside them."

So, in 2009, Lynda and two friends went to Swaziland to begin walking alongside.

"We wanted to see if we could encourage and equip them in what they were already doing. My childhood friend, Lucy Lukhele Kunene, volunteers at the Good Shepherd Hospital. It is a 125-bed facility with an occupancy rate of 182 percent. Additionally, Lucy has more than two dozen orphans coming to her house every day for food, some basic education, and to hear that Jesus loves them. But she has no place to bed them, so they scatter in the bush and return the next day, and the next. So ministry to orphans and sick children was a priority."

Knowing youth education is critical in a nation with the world's highest HIV rate, Lynda had a vision for a youth conference to reach the next generation for Christ. While in Swaziland, she met with Bill's best friend in childhood, Ben Simelane, Lucy's husband, Isaiah, and Elliot Shongwe.

Lynda also held a women's retreat at retired Nazarene missionary Rev. Dana Harding's church, listening to the dreams of sixty women. One attendee, Irene Nxumalo, was a nurse with a vision to run a clinic in Maphiveni (northern Swaziland) in her retirement. The chief had donated a building for the clinic, but Irene needed equipment. Another impediment was the only source of water in the area—a crocodile-infested river. Medicines and a water tank went onto Lynda's list of needs she could try to help meet.

"The Swazis had so many great ministries and ideas but lacked the funds. I began to wonder what one stay-at-home mother could possibly do that would make a difference. God gave me Ephesians 3:20, 'Now to him who is able to do immeasurably more than all we ask or imagine, according to his power that is within us.' In confidence of His sovereignty and provision, HopeAlive268 was born (268 is the telephone area code for Swaziland)."

Lynda shared her passionate vision for Hope-Alive268 and God flung doors open wide. A friend volunteered to make quilts for the hospital. She blogged about it, and soon quilts came in from all over the country. A team of twenty-two volunteers went to Swaziland; five were Lynda's family members: Haven, Joshua, and Kairo Rector; Weston, and Elizabeth. They distributed beautiful quilts, children's books, flip-flops, toothbrushes, and toothpaste; installed new curtains and painted a "Lord is my Shepherd" mural on the walls of Good Shepherd Hospital; ministered to children; led a retreat for one hundred women; installed a water tank; and took medicines for the clinic. They visited two prisons and led thirty women and eighteen juvenile boys to the Lord.

Lynda with orphan at Care Point—Swaziland

Zandile Mavuso, a Nazarene involved in Scripture Union of Swaziland, persuaded the society to change their annual activity date to coordinate with Lynda's team. As a result, more than seven hundred youth attended a dynamic youth rally with teaching on AIDS, music, skits, and evangelistic preaching. In subsequent trips, Lynda's husband, Ricardo Arroyo, has ministered with the men of Swaziland. Today HopeAlive268 is a fully incorporated nonprofit organization. All of the board members in Swaziland are godly Christians. Ministry trips from the US are organized to continue working with orphans (the ministry currently feeds forty to seventy children every day of the year), sprucing up the hospital wards and Nazarene clinic, leading conferences for women, and visiting prisoners. At the Swaziland government's request, in 2013 HopeAlive268 began the process of securing land and housing for ministry to those who have been caught up in human trafficking.

Lynda had the zeal to radically obey God, and she reached thousands with Christ's compassion. Her brother Bill is dedicated to compassionately helping those with schizophrenia and bipolar disorder through research and teaching. Lord willing, they will be educating minds and hearts across two continents for years to come.

6

Worldwide Family

Other things may change us,
but we start and end with family.
—Anthony Brandt

Some of my happiest memories are of climbing trees.
"This branch is mine, that one is yours."

Even when Derek fell out of a tree and broke his
arm, or when I hit a root and scraped all the skin off my
toe, or when Billy got stung with wasps, we kept climb-
ing. We loved spending time in trees, especially the cool-
est one behind Auntie Jo Noonan's house.

We had free rein of the mission field. We wandered
all over, calling out friendly greetings to the Swazis in
the schools, the hospital, across the fields. We explored
creeks, drank the water (I'm still amazed we didn't get
sick), ran along the dusty paths, and dashed in and out
of each other's houses all the time.

It was a lifestyle of innocence that allowed us to roam free and be so incredibly loved and safe. It created an atmosphere where we grew up believing that the world was our family.

* * *

"Mommy, are you going to die on Tuesday?"

When Cynda Whitaker Kindle was preparing for her mastectomy in 2001, it was harder to face her nine-year-old's question than it was to endure the surgery itself. Yet Cynda's response was typical of the dry humor: "Well, I can't guarantee I won't get hit by a bus, but no, I'm not going to die on Tuesday!"

As an active tree-climbing child and a healthy teen who ran track and swam competitively, Cynda never dreamed that she would suffer so much as an adult.

First there was the profoundly sad loss of her son Jeffrey at five months' gestation. Then she was stricken with cancer in her mid-thirties. Because her mother-in-law had died of breast cancer just three months after Cynda had married her husband, Darrell, Cynda opted for a radical mastectomy. Yet three years later Cynda had to have a cancerous thyroid removed. A year after that, doctors discovered cancer in her brain.

"I had heard of people diagnosed with brain tumors who totally lost control of their faculties and couldn't walk or talk. I remember thinking I was going to become a blithering idiot, and my kids would be devastated. I was just lying on my bed, shaking and petrified. I've never been so scared, looking at life as I knew it slipping away.

"Then I remembered that when I was initially diagnosed with cancer my mom had typed 450 Bible verses for me. I got up, still shaking with fear, and pulled out that list. The first one I saw was from Psalm 103: 'Praise the Lord, my soul, and forget not all his benefits—who forgives all your sins and heals all your diseases, who redeems your life from the pit and crowns you with love and compassion, who satisfies your desires with good things so that your youth is renewed like the eagle's' (vv. 2-5).

"Suddenly He was there. No one else can give you consolation when you're diagnosed with a brain tumor. Only God can flood you with peace and stop that shaking. His Word and His presence bring the sweetest comfort."

Cynda battled through nausea, hair loss, and complete exhaustion during weeks of brain radiation. Darrell was by her side through it all. For years she was on continuous treatment with scans every three months to pinpoint the spots still in her chest and neck. She matter-of-factly told people, "If it's progressing, we change medicines. If they're the same, I might get a couple of weeks off from medicines. Pretty much we try to maintain as best we can. And there's new stuff coming out all the time so there are more options to try."

Constant treatment did not slow down this mother of three who works from home as a computer programmer, served for years as church treasurer, sponsored two children in Africa, and, with Darrell, raised three champion Bible quizzers.

Yet she considered her most important ministry to be taking her children to church consistently every week, and she credited her perseverance to her upbringing as a missionary kid.

"I was saved at six and sanctified at ten, and I was raised by the family of God—people who believed in His Word. We hear too much talk about life being gray. God's Word is pretty black and white. If God said it, we've got to do it. What helps me to rely on His promises today is my experience of years on the mission field, where the message of Christianity was not just something I heard but something I saw lived out every day, all the time."

That doesn't mean being an MK was always easy. One of Cynda's challenges was going to boarding school four hundred miles from home. Even though she loved being with friends, she was often homesick. The boarding home had a demerit system that focused on the negative.

Yet God has used even these difficult experiences for good. Cynda learned to focus on the positive. When people asked her when her treatments would be over, she gently broke the news that, barring a miracle, she would be in treatment for the rest of her life. When they asked how she could face that, she cheerfully assured them, "I trust God's plan. I take one day at a time, and God's mercies are 'new every morning'" (Lamentations 3:23).

God's mercy allowed Cynda to go to all her children's Bible quiz meets to cheer them on. Both Gregory and Bethany have been on the National Championship Team (2003, 2009). The three siblings, including younger brother Benjamin, formed a local team that competed at the championships held at Northwest Nazarene University (NNU) in 2008, taking first place. Over eleven years, her children won multiple awards at every level of competition, and Gregory and Bethany have each memorized thirteen books of the New Testament. Bethany also has a great interest in missions and has traveled to the Dominican Republic three times, as well as to Costa Rica, Hungary, Slovenia, Croatia, Austria, Nicaragua, Swaziland, and South Africa.

"Our church, district, and quizzing families have been so supportive of us, but I was amazed at how many missionaries came to the final quiz at General Assembly in 2009 to cheer Bethany's team on to the National Championship. We even had missionaries come to most of their forty-four quizzes at the NNU competition to support them. My missionary aunts and uncles just grab me and hug me whenever I see them. It is just astounding how God has orchestrated this remarkable worldwide family.

"When you consider that on the mission field there were missionaries coming and going, you would think you would feel a sense of loss, but instead you just keep adding to your family. My dad sends out my health updates every three months and it's a great feeling to know that hundreds of people around the world are praying for me. The tremendous irony is that we MKs have this abundance of family because our parents were willing to leave their families.

"My folks have been a wonderful blessing through these years of cancer, but even before that, I was brought up to believe that God can bring miracles. I remember time and again when He would come through for my missionary parents—the car would break down, repairs were $300, money they didn't have, and God would provide. I saw that kind of faith all the time while living on the mission field, and it sustains me today.

"As a child I also saw the burnings of witchcraft paraphernalia in Swaziland, and I am keenly aware of the spiritual battle that is waged. Satan desires for us to live in doubt and fear. But I remember the Swazi Christians as they remained steadfast in very difficult circumstances, and I know God's grace can do the same for me."

Cynda was very grateful that in 2008 God fulfilled her dream to take her children to Swaziland to see where she grew up. They loved the scenery, the wild animals, but most of all, the Swazi people.

Cynda's highlight was reconnecting with an old family friend, Louskin Mabundza, who now oversees all forty Nazarene schools in Swaziland. Her children were able to hear firsthand how abstinence education is making a difference in the AIDS ministries their family has supported over the years.

"My life is enriched because of my exposure as an MK to a different culture and people. I am forever grateful that my parents said *yes* to God. What

Cynda and her children with Louskin

I learned as an MK solidified in me a trust in Christ that is holding fast in the midst of trials and cancer and pain. I also pray that my children will be able to look back on my life and see God's faithfulness. I want them to be able to say, 'No matter what came, she relied on her Savior.'"

Cynda relied on her Savior, right up until May 6, 2012, when she met Him face-to-face and heard Him say, "Well done, My child, so very well done!"

Author's note: Cynda and I would likely never have met if our parents had not said yes to God and gone to serve Him in Swaziland. Her friendship was one of the greatest gifts God has given me, and I miss her very much. I am so thankful we got to play together with our Swazi friends, to have tea parties under the trees, to run barefoot and make grass forts and cars out of wire, to wander into each other's homes freely, to giggle at sleepovers and whisper secrets under the covers. We were more than friends, we were family, as so many fellow MKs become.

When we were children and another MK child, Leeann Bach, was killed in a car accident, Cynda told her mom, "Leeann's so lucky. She gets to see Jesus. I'll be so glad when I get to see Jesus." Then her eyes filled with tears as she said, "Oh, Mommy, I love Jesus with all my heart!"

Cynda lived her whole life loving Jesus with all her heart. She was a remarkable person whose faithfulness and commitment to Christ personified how to live a victorious life with great courage. She never turned from the narrow path, even when the mountains were steep and the valleys low. Cynda's life amplified the truth that glorifying God is the highest achievement we can ever attain. Those of us who knew her were incredibly privileged—and we'll be so pleased to introduce her to you in heaven.

7

Global Worldview

*Sometimes it's the smallest decisions
that can change your life forever.*
—Keri Russell

*Our parents always gave us a great sense that we
were part of their team—that we were not just there as
children but as part of God's plan. We always knew we
had a role to play in the ministry; we were needed and
doing our part. Even though at times we were away in
boarding school, their expressions of value and including
us contributed to our personhood and sense of security.
We mattered to them.*

We mattered to God.

* * *

Sara Cunningham Falk and her husband, Joshua,
decided to do something different as newlyweds in

Sara and Josh Falk and son Lincoln

2005: they went to Africa. Not for a honeymoon, but to spend two years in Sierra Leone, the country that was then rated as the worst place in the world to live. Married for just three months, Joshua and Sara plunged into a world with no electricity, no running water, and no refrigerator in their tiny house.

"I grew up in South Africa, Kenya, and Madagascar. Joshua lived in Swaziland and Côte d'Ivoire and did a short-term missions stint with Samaritan's Purse. We thought we were prepared for Sierra Leone. We thought wrong."

Sara and Joshua worked by candlelight. Laundry took hours, washing the clothes by hand and hanging them to dry. They drank powdered milk. Meat was outrageously expensive and chicken banned due to bird flu. Sara used propane gas for cooking and went to the market almost daily for fresh food. But the biggest challenge was water.

"Every day we had to take buckets to find water. First, we had to find a tap that was working. There were lines and lines and lines, usually of children doing the chore for their families. We had to boil the water. I would boil it, cool it, run it through our water filter, then start all over again with a new batch. It was a constant activity throughout my day."

Nevertheless, Joshua and Sara's volunteer efforts made a difference. Joshua worked extensively with the JESUS Film ministry, training leaders and showing the films. Both Joshua and Sara taught theological education. Sara also worked with finances.

"I trained church treasurers. They had nothing, so we gave them pencils, paper, and a small calculator. I taught how to keep track of what comes in on Sunday and goes out during the week. It was challenging!"

Yet those challenges paled in light of what Sierra Leone had suffered from the illegal diamond trade and civil war.

"You could see the effects everywhere—including people with body parts missing from warfare. It is horrific what they have been through. You could stop anyone on the road and they could tell you an incredible story of survival. People kept telling us about the movie *Blood Diamond*, but we couldn't watch it. For us, the story was too real.

"During those difficult days, my parents were an inspiration and wonderful prayer partners. A highlight was our weekly Skype call from a cybercafe. Dad was amazingly positive and would remind us that in every circumstance there is always something to learn, and there is always something to teach someone else.

"One thing we learned was that the hope for Sierra Leone comes from people like George Cole. His entire family—except for one sister—was killed. George sold cheap shoes to survive. After finding Christ, George helped show the JESUS Film. Using a megaphone, he would enthusiastically and loudly proclaim, 'Come and see Jesus!' He was so full of joy, and hurting people were drawn to that."

Though Sara and Joshua both grew up as MKs in Africa, they met at Nazarene Theological Seminary. Joshua earned his master's degree in divinity and Sara a master of arts in intercultural studies.

Joshua is Canadian and Sara American by birth, so they continue to blend cultures, just as they learned to do as children. Sara first learned to blend cultures when her Afrikaner friends refused to play with her because her family invited Xhosas, from the Bantu ethnic group of South Africa, into their home.

"Experiences like this give you a global worldview. So when something in the world happens, you have a frame of reference. It creates a greater empathy for suffering and calls you to action and to prayer. Even today when I enter a new community or church, I gravitate to people who don't fit in, who need some extra love."

Sara's gifts come in handy with Joshua's call to ministry that he received as a nine-year-old listening to Lenora Pease, a missionary to India. After the adventure in Sierra Leone, Joshua has served as an associate and an interim senior pastor, and was ordained in 2009. Because the young couple has seen poverty up close, every couple of months they walk through their home and give away what they don't need.

"In Sierra Leone we saw Christians who had been through a terrible war, had limbs chopped off, and had so little—yet they were amazingly thankful. We went to give of our lives to them, yet they gave us a legacy: Every night before we go to sleep, we share with each other three things we are especially grateful for, and we thank God together."

Joshua and Sara have a passion to help others, including their own sons, Lincoln and Owen, acquire a global worldview. So does Sara's sister, Jessica, who went to a creative access country for a summer with Youth in Mission.

"I went over to learn the language, which we did three days a week. The other two days we hung out with new friends, learning the culture and witnessing. One person was interested in learning more about Jesus but was petrified to talk with me because I was a Christian. If he was caught, he could be arrested or even tortured. It was an eye-opener. Yet even with our cultures and ethnicities being so different, our needs are the same. We all desire to be loved and accepted, to be safe, to care for our families . . . we all need Jesus."

Jessica graduated from Northwest Nazarene University with a degree in business administration and an emphasis in global business. Soon after, she met her husband, Matt Craig, as they both worked for Walmart in Arkansas. Their first date was to go to a friend's farm and grill their dinner in the back of a pick-up truck. Another memorable meal together was on James Bond Island during their honeymoon in

Thailand. They lived in Asia for two-and-a-half years when they both accepted jobs with Lotus (similar to Walmart) in Shanghai, China.

"Growing up as an MK, learning to adapt and to be flexible, has been invaluable to me in the business world. My best friend in South Africa was Indian, and I went to school with Afrikaners, Xhosa, and British friends. I was in boarding school in Germany for a year, hanging out with Americans, Canadians, and Europeans. At boarding school in Kenya, we also had Kenyan, Danish, Korean, and Finnish friends, and I also got to know the Malagasy people when we lived in Madagascar. So I learned the skill of the chameleon—cultural adaptation—and that is a huge benefit in global business."

Jessica trained their buyers in corporate research and development. All the training was in English, but the meetings were in Chinese.

"The written language is complex, but the verbal wasn't too bad. There are four different tones for the same word. I didn't know all the tones, but if I spoke fast and put words in context with other words, they could understand.

"Culturally, I was trying to blend African-Chinese-American. For instance, in Africa when you gain weight, people tell you it is wonderful. In China, friends will caution you if you are getting too fat. In the US, your friends may just ignore your weight. But while the different cultures have differing views to something like that, in all three cultures, family is important."

Matt and Jessica's daughter Kaley was born in China. Her "ayi" (aunt) helped Jessica to learn Chinese, and Jessica taught her some English. They also shared Christ with people, giving away Bibles that Jessica's parents brought when they visited. Jessica feels strongly about the importance of resourcing people with knowledge—spiritually and academically.

"I spent a summer volunteering in East Africa. I traveled to Rwanda, Ethiopia, and the Democratic Republic of Congo. I met people who have suffered. But I also saw that much bloodshed has been avoided because of the courage, tenacity, and forgiveness of Christians. This is spiritual wisdom. I also saw educated individuals working to support extended families. That is freedom from poverty."

Jessica and Matt have a goal to support as many scholarships as they can to educate people toward freedom and wisdom. Now back in the US from China, they are thankful, along with Kaley and her new sisters Madison and Mackenzie, to be worshipping in a Nazarene church again.

"People from every culture want to feel welcomed and accepted. When you can create that kind of atmosphere in a church, it speaks volumes about who we are as Christians. We tell people the Church of the Nazarene is 'one size fits all.' It welcomes all, loves all, preaches the Hope for all."

Only MKs like Sara and Jessica can truthfully make statements like, "We drove to six countries in one day because Mom took a wrong turn in Italy." Today their lives are continually moving in the right direction—loving God, loving others.

8

World Advocate

You really can change the world if you care enough.
—Marian Wright Edelman

We were walking into one of the beautiful gorges in Swaziland. As I put my foot down, I was aware of something that looked multicolored, but I didn't realize what it was until my foot actually landed on it. At that point my friends said I jumped back about ten feet and began yelling "SNAKE!" Fortunately it was not a fast-moving mamba or puff adder, but a well-fed, sleeping boa constrictor—so I lived to tell the story.

* * *

At the age of nine a glimpse into the eyes of a Swazi boy rocked Dr. Robert (Rob) Gailey's world and changed the direction of his life.

"I was riding in the car with my parents when I saw a boy walking along the road in the dust. He was dressed in rags, and as we passed, my eyes looked into his. Suddenly I realized how different our lives were. What separated the two of us? Why was I born into a life of riding in cars and he was born to walk dusty roads?

"I stared out the window for a long time. I began to comprehend that I could drive to see their lives, but they could not drive to see my life. I could make complex and diverse choices, and could even, to some extent, recreate myself through education or other life changes—yet many could not even choose their own food, school, or transportation. Why did I have an overabundance of choices when others had none?"

This revelation marked the beginning of Rob's lifelong quest to be an advocate for poor people by increasing their choices through poverty alleviation.

As a child in Swaziland, Rob was considered "rich." Children wanted to play with his toys and touch his clothes and even envied his toothbrush.

Then as a teenager in the US, people constantly lauded his family for having been willing to live in poverty in Africa. Many gave them gifts or money because they were "so poor."

During high school Rob gravitated to the world of business. He purchased stock and dreamed of becoming an investment banker, telling God he was willing to be a witness to the wealthy. Yet throughout these years Rob could not quite shake the mental image of looking into the eyes of a boy in rags walking along a dusty road.

"I kept asking why I was born into a loving home with educated parents, given the incredible privilege of being a missionary kid, an opportunity to be educated and become whatever I wanted . . . and he was not. I kept feeling the tug of Luke 12:48, which basically says: to whom much is given, much shall be required."

At a critical time in Rob's life, his senior year of high school, his parents returned to the mission field.

"Once again confronted with stark poverty, I was broken by the things that break the heart of God. God was teaching me that the very business principles that so enamored me could be used to teach others to climb out of poverty."

Rob enrolled at Eastern Nazarene College. During his freshman year he heard missionary Dr. John Nielson speak in chapel about a call to full-time ministry. Rob committed to a lifetime of working within and through the church to help reduce poverty in the world. He was also influenced by his classmates, MK Dr. Jamie Gates, who is now professor of sociology and director of Center for Justice and Reconciliation at PLNU, and Larry Bollinger, who is now director of Nazarene Compassionate Ministries (NCM) International.

After graduating summa cum laude with a business degree, Rob went to Nazarene Theological Seminary for a missiology degree. He soon switched to a master's of divinity degree.

"I began to see the importance of theology in poverty alleviation. It is not only that we need to enable people to have more choices. More choices can also lead to bad choices, like gambling instead of paying school fees. I began to recognize that the uniqueness of *Christian* economic development is that we offer wisdom that encourages people to make life-affirming, others-centered choices. The Church in richer cultures also needs this wisdom—for example, to encourage members to support a poverty alleviation program rather than buy a new boat."

While working on his master's degree, Rob and his wife, Wanda, were asked to serve for eighteen months as missionaries to Malawi. Rob served as interim director of the Nazarene Vocational School there. Since pastors are unpaid in many developing countries, the school taught pastors skills to become bivocational. While in Malawi Rob first became interested in microfinance, the practice of providing small loans to poor entrepreneurs in the developing world.

After graduating from seminary, Rob was soon working with many of the leading experts and pioneers in this movement as research director of the Microcredit Summit Campaign in Washington, D.C., and later as director of Microfinance Consulting Services for World Relief, a Christian nonprofit organization. He launched a global discussion group and participated in other collaborative workgroups around the issue of poverty measurement tools and their use within microfinance institutions. Rob soon discovered that the global perspective he brought to the table was unique because of the worldview he had developed as a missionary kid.

"As a preteen I was the same kid with exactly the same resources in both Swaziland and the US—yet in Swaziland I was considered uber-rich and in the US I was looked on as dirt poor. I also thought Swazi pastors were poor until I went to Malawi. In Swaziland, when I ate at a pastor's home there was usually a tablecloth and Western-style eating utensils. In Malawi we often ate meals with our fingers and sometimes sat on the floor. From these experiences and others I came to understand that defining poverty is often shaped by what people see, compared to what they have themselves—and not to a larger reality."

Today Rob is an associate professor of business at Point Loma Nazarene University (PLNU) and the director of the Center for International Development, which applies life-affirming business principles and practices to the complex challenges of global poverty. He teaches nonprofit management, social entrepreneurship, and theories of economic development.

"Once my friends and I were building a fort," Rob teaches in one illustration from his childhood as an MK. "As we gathered branches from trees a Swazi lady scolded us for wasting good firewood. Though I didn't realize it at the time, I was learning that a plaything for me was a matter of livelihood for them."

"When I was in college I was challenged by an almost unbelievable statistic: forty thousand children were dying every day from hunger and preventable diseases. Today that number is down to eighteen thousand per day. But no Christian should be comfortable until that number reaches zero.

"Microfinance has played a role in helping that number drop by twenty-two thousand a day. Microfinance empowers women to have access to more resources. Studies have shown that when a woman is educated and empowered and gains access to more resources, her kids are better fed and more likely to attend school—and often the entire community benefits. Yet even though microfinance is a powerful transformational tool, I am always in search of more effective solutions to alleviate poverty."

Rob's goal is to make Christlike disciples, mentor others, and inspire students to help with international development. He encourages students to use their best gifts and skills while they are young. "Don't wait until you've made a lot of money and then write a check. Use your minds, connections, and best ideas now to address—and help the Church address—the complex challenges of poverty."

Because of Professor Gailey's influence, students have traveled to volunteer in various countries as well as at Hope International in Lancaster, Pennsylvania, a nonprofit ministry that specializes in microfinance.

In 2013 Rob used his sabbatical to help Nazarene Compassionate Ministries on a project. He and his family traveled for six months to ten countries in Africa and Asia to look into child development programs. They helped NCM develop an improved data collection process for children ministered to by the church.

Rob has also taken students—and sometimes his own family—on trips to Mexico and Armenia to

Dr. Rob Gailey and family in Africa

help build affordable, energy-efficient homes. These buildings are made from polystyrene foam blocks so light that even children can carry them, and then filled with cement. Using this type of construction material provides excellent insulation, durability, and seismic stability against earthquakes.

On one recent trip Rob's team constructed seven buildings for the Nazarene seminary in Tecate, Mexico.

"It's essential for us to see the importance of the Church, and to be engaged in a local congregation where we will be challenged to live out both personal and social holiness under an umbrella of accountability before God and one another. Church leaders must be prophetic voices who, in their respective cultures, encourage and live out holistic lifestyle transformation. The next generation needs to be exposed to socioeconomic differences in this world and to train their hearts and minds to be engaged as the Church in caring for people who live in poverty."

Rob Gailey is a product of Nazarene missions and Nazarene higher education. He is revitalizing the Church by highlighting our roots in Wesley and Bresee's emphases in holistic ministry—in light of our twenty-first-century context.

Epilogue
World Changers

How wonderful it is that nobody need wait a single moment before starting to change the world.
—Anne Frank

I feel tremendously blessed and privileged to have had the kind of life I have had. It's not a scary thing, this MK life, it's a wonderful thing.
—Sara Cunningham Falk

* * *

Most missionary kids will admit it was a challenge growing up on the cusp of multiple cultures. Their childhoods roamed among worlds, nomadic and global. Yet those MK experiences also forged in them a strong biblical worldview that produced remarkable perspectives and unique gifts. As they resonate with their multicultural heritage, it propels them to change their world.

The stories in this book are just a tiny slice of the wonderful Nazarene MKs from all over the globe who are changing our world in meaningful ways. In fact, there are so many missionary kids involved in the Church and various other ministries that if we wrote down all their stories, no doubt it would fill bookshelves. There have been—or are—missionary kids who have served the Church as regional directors, pastors, international NCM coordinator, both short-term and career missionaries, vice-president of the Nazarene Foundation, caring Sunday school teachers, translators, local church leaders, mission field directors, district superintendents, professors at Nazarene universities, a general superintendent, and a general superintendent's spouse.

There are also MKs serving as committed laypeople in countless churches, impacting their world through a vivid Christian witness in professions of law, neonatal nursing, teaching, banking, speech therapy, broadcasting, and many more.

These are the children of parents who dared to live in the center of God's will. Their lives are a rich legacy of Nazarene global missions. We know them as missionary kids.

And world changers.

Call to Action
Change the World

*Christians are supposed to not merely
endure change but to cause it.*
—Harry Emerson Fosdick

- Pray for individuals called to missionary service to have the courage to say yes to God.
- Pray specifically for missionaries to have peace about their children's futures.
- Pray for God to forge a foundational, life-changing Christian worldview in the life of each missionary kid.
- Pray for missionary families.
- Be involved in your local LINKS program.
- When you have missionary families come to your church, take time to talk with the MKs.
- For a greater understanding of MKs, read the excellent book *Third Culture Kids* by David C. Pollack and Ruth E. Van Reken.

- If you live near a college, invest time and interest in a young adult MK. You might be able to significantly help them to adapt to the local culture.
- Ask God how He can use YOU to change the world.

Pronunciation Guide

Chapter 2

Magagula	Muh-gah-GOO-luh
Shongwe	Shong-weh
Mfundisi	M-foon-DEE-see
Pato	Puh-toh

Chapter 5

Lukhele	Lew-ke-leh
Kunene	Koo-NAY-nee
Simelane	Sim-ee-lah-nee
Nxumalo	Koo-mah-loh
Maphiveni	Mah-pee-VAY-nee

Chapter 6

Mabundza	Mah-boon-dzah